NATURAL WORLD

DOLPHIN

HABITATS • LIFE CYCLES • FOOD CHAINS • THREATS

Nic Davies

RAINTREE
STECK-VAUGHN
RSVP PUBLISHERS

A Harcourt Company

Austin   New York
www.steck-vaughn.com

NATURAL WORLD

Chimpanzee • Crocodile • Dolphin • Elephant
Giant Panda • Great White Shark • Grizzly Bear
Hippopotamus • Killer Whale • Lion • Orangutan
Penguin • Polar Bear • Tiger

Cover: Eye to eye with a bottle-nosed dolphin
Title page: A dolphin gives the camera a friendly glance.
Contents page: This dolphin is using its tail to rise above the waves.
Index page: A pair of dolphins swimming off the coast of the Bahamas

Published by Raintree Steck-Vaughn Publishers, an imprint of Steck-Vaughn Company

Library of Congress Cataloging-in-Publication Data
Davies, Nic.
Dolphin / Nic Davies.
     p.   cm.—(Natural world)
     Includes bibliographical references and index.
     ISBN 0-7398-2766-9 (hard)
     0-7398-3125-9 (soft)
     1. Dolphins—Juvenile literature.
     [1. Dolphins.]
     I. Title. II. Series.

Printed in Italy. Bound in the United States.
1 2 3 4 5 6 7 8 9 0 04 03 02 01 00

Picture acknowledgments
Bruce Coleman 7 (Ken Balcomb), 12 (Carl Roessler), 16 (Jeff Foott), 22 (Jane Burton), 48 (Jeff Foott); Nic Davies 35; Digital Vision 39, 40, 41; FLPA/Earthviews *front cover*; NHPA 6 (Roger Tidman), 8 (Laurie Campbell), 10 (Gerard Lacz), 26 (Norbert Wu), 29 (Gerard Lacz), 30 (Norbert Wu), 32 (Kelvin Aitken); Oxford Scientific Films 13, 14 (Konrad Wothe), 15 (Daniel J. Cox), 20 (Kim Westerskov), 33 (D. G. Fox), 34 (Kathie Atkinson), 36 (David B. Fleetham), 43, 44 middle, 45 bottom (Konrad Wothe). Science Photo Library 37 (Dolphin Institute); Still Pictures 1 (Robert Henno), 17 (Horst Schafer), 19, 21 (Roland Seitre), 28 (H. Ausloos), 38 (M. and C. Denis-Hoot), 42 (Mark Carwardine), 44 bottom (Host Schafer), 45 top (H. Ausloos); The Stock Market 11 (Craig Tuttle) 18; Tony Stone 3 (Tim Davis); Tom Walmsley 9, 27, 31, 44 top. Map on page 4 by Victoria Webb. All other artworks by Michael Posen.

Contents

Meet the Dolphin

Dolphins are air-breathing mammals, just like us, but they spend their entire lives in water. There are many different species of dolphins, and millions of individuals. Dolphins live in oceans, seas, lakes, and rivers throughout the world. They usually live in groups called schools, herds, or pods. The most popular of all dolphins is the bottle-nosed, which is famous for its friendliness toward people. It is also the dolphin most commonly kept in marine aquariums.

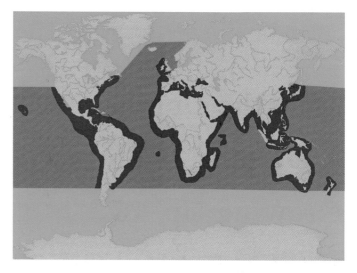

▲ The bright red shading on this map shows where most bottle-nosed dolphins live.

DOLPHIN FACTS

The bottle-nosed dolphin got its name because the shape of its beak reminded people of old-fashioned bottles. It also has a scientific name, which is *Tursiops truncatus*.

●

Males grow slightly larger than females and can reach nearly 14 ft. (4.3 m) in length and weigh 1,400 lbs. (635 kg) or more.

▶ An adult bottle-nosed dolphin leaping from the water

Dorsal fin
This hook-shaped, boneless fin acts like the keel of a boat. It helps prevent the dolphin from rolling in the water.

Skin
The smooth skin is very sensitive. The skin secretes an oily substance that may help the dolphin to pass more easily through the water.

Blowhole
This is the dolphin's nostril. It is sealed with a muscular flap of skin to keep out water when the dolphin is not taking a breath.

Melon
This fatty bulge in the forehead helps to focus the sounds the dolphin uses to hunt and to communicate.

Body
The torpedo-shaped body, more than one-third of which is muscle, gives the dolphin a smooth swimming action.

Beak
The bottle-nosed dolphin's beak, or snout, is shorter than those in many other dolphin species.

Flippers (pectoral fins)
These are used for steering and for communicating by touch.

Eyes
Each eye can move independently. This gives the dolphin excellent vision both above and below the surface.

Blubber
Below the skin is a layer of fat called blubber. It keeps the cold out and acts as an energy store.

Tail
The tail, with its two boneless fins, called flukes, is used for swimming. It is moved up and down, not from side to side like a fish's tail.

◀ A humpback whale feeds by taking a huge gulp of water. It then pushes it out through its horny baleen plates to strain out the food.

▼ Orcas are toothed cetaceans. They hunt a wide variety of sea animals, including seals, dolphins, whales, penguins, and squid.

The Cetacean Family

Dolphins and their close cousins, whales and porpoises, are together known as cetaceans (pronounced "seh-tay-shuns"). This family of aquatic mammals includes the largest animal on Earth—the mighty blue whale, which can reach more than 100 ft. (31 m) long and weigh 200 tons.

Scientists have discovered 81 cetacean species, but there are probably more. Of these, 35 are true dolphins, including the largest dolphin, the orca (also known as the killer whale). Some dolphins live in family groups. Others, particularly ocean-living dolphins, may gather by the thousands. Dolphins are also found far up some rivers in warmer parts of the world. For example, some live in the Amazon River in South America and the Ganges, Indus, and Yangtze rivers in Asia.

There are two main types of cetaceans. Some, such as the blue whale, have special filters in their mouths, called baleen plates. These plates strain out food from the sea. Other cetaceans, such as the sperm whale, have teeth to catch their prey. Dolphins are toothed cetaceans. This book will tell you about the life cycle of one of them—the bottle-nosed dolphin.

DOLPHIN ANCESTORS

All land animals have evolved from animals that lived in the sea. However, more than 50 million years ago, a meat-eating wolflike animal with hooves gave up its life on land and returned to the water. Over time, its shape changed to suit its new watery home. One result is the dolphin family, whose closest land relatives are hoofed animals, such as cows. Some dolphins still have useless hind-leg bones under their skin.

A Dolphin Is Born

A dolphin mother is ready to give birth about twelve months after mating. Some mothers prefer to give birth in the relative calm and safety of coastal waters. But many have their young, called calves, out in the open sea. Female bottle-nosed dolphins usually have only one calf. Twins are rare and unlikely to survive.

The young of mammals are usually born headfirst, but a dolphin calf is normally born tail-first. The calf's tail flukes and dorsal fin are floppy, which makes its birth easier. They soon become firm.

▲ A mother and her calf breathe together at the surface. A newborn calf finds breathing difficult at first. It has to take many more breaths than its mother.

▶ A dolphin calf swims through the waves with its mother. The calf is fully formed at birth and can swim right away.

A CHILLING BIRTH

The unborn calf is cozy in its mother's womb at a constant temperature of 98.6° F (37° C). But the sea water outside is much colder. The newborn calf cannot afford to be shocked by this temperature difference, because it has to rush to the surface immediately and take its first breath. Its mother helps by urging the calf upward with her head, beak, or flippers.

The newborn dolphin calf may weigh as much as 45 lbs. (20 kg) and be more than 3 ft. (1 m) long—more than one-third the length of its mother!

The calf feeds on its mother's milk about one hour after being born. Then it eats at least four times an hour. Although the calf doesn't yet have teeth to get in the way, its lack of flexible lips means it cannot suckle. So the mother nurses her calf by squirting her milk into the calf's mouth.

Early Days

The bottle-nosed mother tries to protect her new calf, which is only interested in feeding as much as possible. To make feeding easier, the mother sometimes rolls her body on its side. This means the calf doesn't have to swim underneath to reach the teats on her mammary glands.

For at least the first week, the mother and calf are never apart. During this time, she doesn't hunt. The calf saves energy by swimming close to her side, so it gets pulled along in her slipstream.

▶ Nourished by its mother's fat-rich milk, a young dolphin gains weight rapidly.

▼ Swimming at its mother's side may help to camouflage the young calf. It makes its shape less obvious to predators such as sharks and orcas.

DOLPHIN MILK

A dolphin mother's milk contains more than five times as much fat as human milk. The young calf feeds from both of its mother's mammary glands, each of which has a single teat. The teats are hidden away in her belly until feeding time.

Apart from its small size, a newborn calf is easy to spot. Its skin is paler than normal, and it may have vertical stripes, called fetal folds, on its body. The stripes are caused by the way the calf's large body is folded up in the womb before birth.

Some calves are born with whiskers on their beaks, but they usually lose them after a few weeks or months. The function of the whiskers is unclear. They may be important for touch. Having whiskers may help the bottle-nosed calf to stay in close contact with its mother at night or in cloudy water.

Babysitting

The calf depends on its mother's milk for its first twelve to eighteen months. For the mother to feed herself and produce enough milk for her calf, she has to catch nearly one-tenth of her own body weight in food each day. The calf is at risk from predators, such as great white sharks or orcas, if it is left alone.

Pregnant females and mothers with young calves usually travel together in groups, called bands. The females are often related, and the close bonds between them encourage them to care for all the calves. They do this by taking turns babysitting the young calves while the others hunt.

▲ Great white sharks prey on unprotected bottle-nosed calves if they get the chance. Tight-knit bands of dolphins, in which all the females help to guard the young, may help to keep prowling sharks at bay.

▶ Groups of related females cooperate closely in looking after the calves. Males are thought to play no part in rearing the young dolphins.

"Midwife" dolphins may help with the birth of a new calf. They bite through the umbilical cord between a mother and her calf. "Aunt" dolphins guide the calf to the surface for its first breath, while "nurses" feed calves that are not their own. One female may act as aunt, midwife, and nurse.

The young calf gradually becomes more and more adventurous. After just a few weeks, it starts to spend some time on its own.

WHISTLE YOUR NAME

Soon after birth, a mother whistles to her calf. At first the whistle is just a single, steady note. But it quickly develops into a complex sound, called a signature whistle. The calf will use this as its "name" for the rest of its life. Older dolphins can copy these whistles and often mimic each other's calls.

13

Infanticide

One of the biggest dangers to many young mammals is a deadly attack by an adult of the same species. This is called infanticide.

Adult bottle-nosed dolphins sometimes kill harbor porpoises. Scientists have noticed that the dead porpoises have injuries similar to those of some dead bottle-nosed calves found on beaches. This may be evidence of infanticide, with bottle-nosed males killing calves. Infanticide may occur because an adult male hopes that if he kills a calf, its mother will mate with him to get a new calf.

PROTECTING CALVES

A female bottle-nosed dolphin usually mates with several different males. This may help to protect her calf against infanticide. When the calf is born twelve months later, none of the males will be sure whether or not he is the father of her calf. If he kills the calf, he risks killing his own offspring.

◄ A young calf may be at risk from adult bottle-nosed males, as well as from predators. The males may kill porpoises to practice killing dolphin calves.

Even if infanticide does occur, the dolphin society is generally extremely protective. There are many records of dolphins helping not only fellow dolphins but also other species, including humans.

▼ A bottle-nosed dolphin has between 78 and 102 cone-shaped teeth. An adult may use its teeth to attack other cetaceans, leaving long scratch marks called rakes. The worst injuries occur when the dolphin uses its beak as a battering ram, or its tail as a club.

Growing Up

The relationship between a mother bottle-nosed dolphin and her calf may last for six years or more. Being together for so long allows the mother to teach the youngster about its habitat, where and how to find food, and how to behave toward other dolphins.

▼ The calf lives with its mother in a band of females. It learns quickly about the relationships and rules that govern dolphin society.

▲ A mother and an older calf touch beaks to reinforce social bonds. Even when it is independent, the calf will still be able to identify its mother in a large school by listening for her signature whistle.

Weaning begins at four months. Although the calf starts to eat solid food, such as fish or squid, it will usually continue nursing for at least another year. Sometimes, nursing continues for several years. Perhaps this is to provide extra food in the calf's early independence, or to reinforce the bond between mother and calf.

Growth is rapid. By eighteen months old, the calf has doubled its length and quadrupled its weight. Early growth is important in all marine mammals. The bigger or fatter the animal becomes, the less heat it will lose to the cold water around it.

World of Sound

Because of the weird and wonderful sounds dolphins make—from buzzes, squawks, and clicks to yelps and pops—the dolphin calf grows up in a world that is never quiet.

Visibility underwater is not good, because light travels poorly in even the clearest waters. Sound, on the other hand, travels much faster and farther in water than it does in air. To make the most of their aquatic home, dolphins have developed excellent hearing and the ability to use sound underwater.

◀ A dolphin has a tiny ear opening on each side of its head, just behind the eye. It may be that these ear openings can hear only sounds above the water's surface. Vital underwater sounds travel to the dolphin's inner ear through its jawbone, not through the outer ear openings.

Dolphins use clicklike sounds mainly to hunt and explore their surroundings. Whistles, squeaks, and other sounds are used to communicate. For example, they may "blow" their signature whistles in different ways to mean different things. A dolphin may whistle "I'm Bob ...." But by making its whistle louder or shorter, it may also be saying "... and I'm frightened." It is possible that dolphins also use sounds to represent objects, such as fish.

Dolphins can also send signals by hitting their bodies against the water's surface. A belly flop may be a greeting to dolphins far away. A tail slap may mean "I'm angry; stay away." Each signal may mean something different in a different situation.

▲ Nobody knows how dolphins make their clicking sounds. But they may use both the larynx (voice box) and the nasal passages (situated below the blowhole). The blowhole does not breathe out air while the dolphin is making its clicking sounds.

Family and Friends

Schools of bottle-nosed dolphins vary in size from a few individuals to several hundred. The largest gatherings are simply many smaller groups made up of families, friends, or temporary companions.

Between three and six years of age, the calf, now called a juvenile, becomes largely independent of its mother. It has to find food for itself. By now the mother may be pregnant again or even have a new calf. She encourages her older calf's independence, but their relationship remains close. If a new calf dies, the older calf may even begin nursing again.

◄ Aside from a few close family members, a dolphin school may vary from day to day.

The juvenile slowly replaces its mother's company with that of other juveniles. Many of them were reared by the same band of females. The juveniles join subadult groups, which are usually either all-male "bachelor" groups or mixed-sex groups. Occasionally, females form a "girls-only" subadult group.

▼ Playing together is an important part of life in dolphin society. Groups of dolphins enjoy nothing better than surfing the waves.

Aside from the dangerous few weeks following birth, this early independence is the most difficult time in a dolphin's life. The pressures of building social status, avoiding predators, and having to fend for themselves leads many to the brink of starvation. Sadly, the death toll is high.

Hunter and Hunted

During adolescence, young dolphins use the hunting skills taught to them by their mothers and other band members. The young dolphins' choice of prey is important if they are to survive to adulthood. They must learn to avoid harmful species, such as the poisonous scorpion fish or lionfish found in the tropics.

Dolphins must also choose prey that provides lots of fat or protein, such as mackerel or mullet, for the least amount of hunting effort. There is no point in using more energy to catch a fish than the fish contains. If a dolphin makes too many bad decisions, it will starve.

▼ Dolphins seem to be able to distinguish between fish that are nutritious, such as these mullet, and those that provide little nourishment.

DOLPHIN FOOD CHAIN

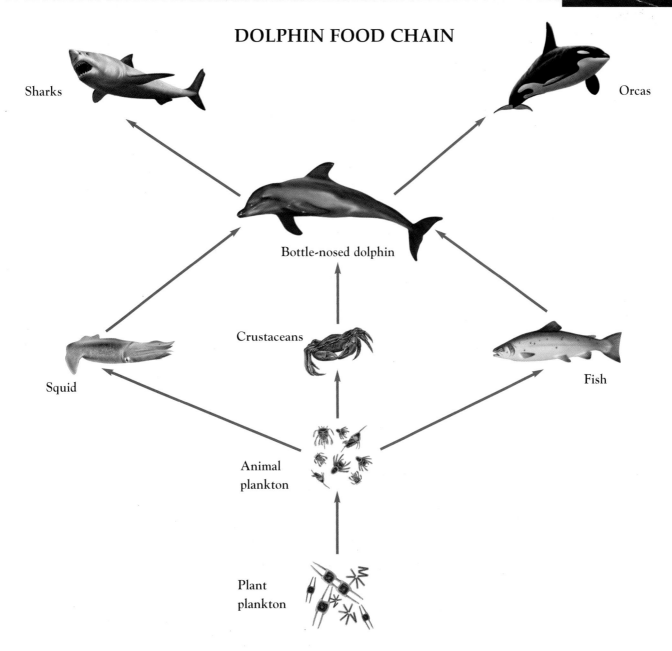

Sharks

Orcas

Bottle-nosed dolphin

Crustaceans

Squid

Fish

Animal plankton

Plant plankton

Adult dolphins are sometimes preyed upon by orcas and sharks. This includes the great white shark and the tiger shark. However, bottle-nosed dolphins are large compared to other dolphins, so these attacks are probably rare. Bottle-nosed dolphins sometimes even attack sharks to drive them away.

▲ At the bottom of the bottle-nosed dolphin's food chain are tiny living things called plankton.

Seeing with Sound

Humans live in a world of light, so sight has become our most important sense. But because dolphins live in a murky, underwater world, they have developed a method of "seeing" with sound. This amazing ability is called echolocation. Dolphins use it to find food and to navigate.

The dolphin makes a pulse of sound called an echolocation click. It then waits for an echo. If it hears an echo, it knows that the click has bounced back off an object in the water. The longer it takes to hear an echo, the farther away the object is. If there is no echo, the dolphin knows there's nothing there.

▼ This cross section of a dolphin's head shows where the clicks might be produced and how they are transmitted.

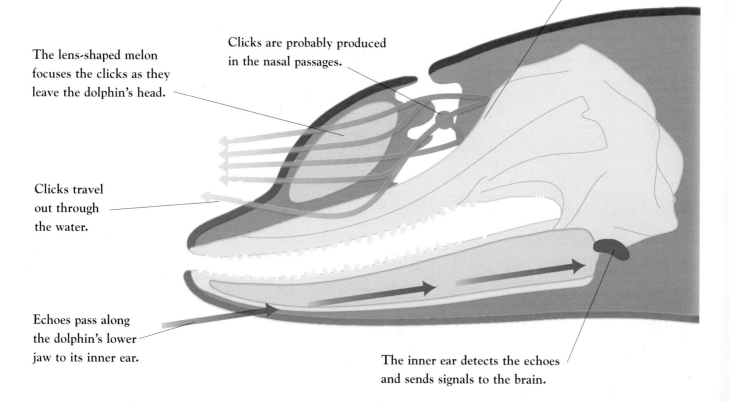

The dish-shaped skull also helps to focus the clicks.

The lens-shaped melon focuses the clicks as they leave the dolphin's head.

Clicks are probably produced in the nasal passages.

Clicks travel out through the water.

Echoes pass along the dolphin's lower jaw to its inner ear.

The inner ear detects the echoes and sends signals to the brain.

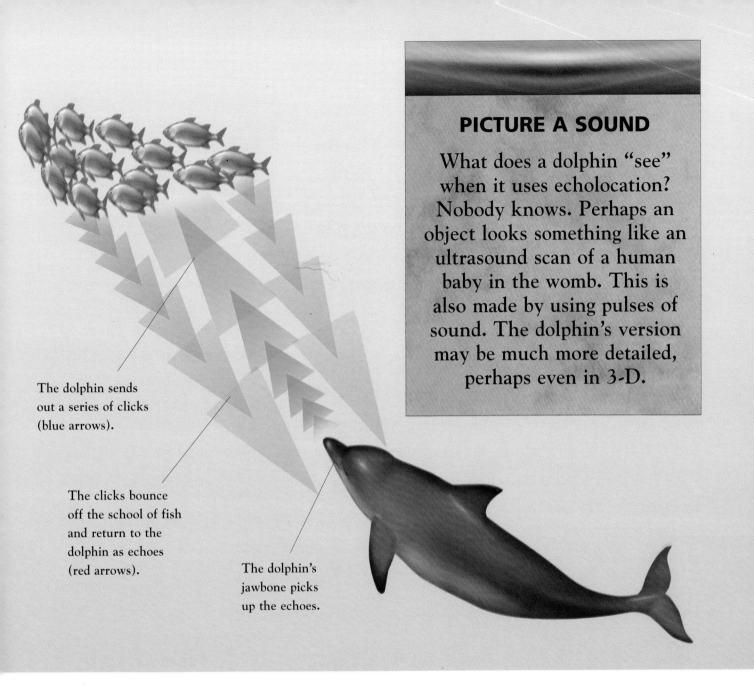

PICTURE A SOUND

What does a dolphin "see" when it uses echolocation? Nobody knows. Perhaps an object looks something like an ultrasound scan of a human baby in the womb. This is also made by using pulses of sound. The dolphin's version may be much more detailed, perhaps even in 3-D.

The dolphin sends out a series of clicks (blue arrows).

The clicks bounce off the school of fish and return to the dolphin as echoes (red arrows).

The dolphin's jawbone picks up the echoes.

The dolphin's echolocation is probably much more complicated than this. We can only guess what information it provides. Hundreds of clicks can be made in a fraction of a second, detecting objects more than 300 ft. (100 m) away. Some scientists think that dolphins may be able to use powerful echolocation clicks to stun fish. The clicks may also tell them whether a female dolphin is pregnant.

▲ Some parts of a fish's body return echoes better than others. So this dolphin may be seeing a school of body parts rather than whole fish.

Finding Food

Bottle-nosed dolphins eat mainly fish and squid, which they catch with their pointed teeth. Occasionally they will eat crustaceans such as shrimps. Dolphins need to do a lot of hunting to survive. A 165-lb. (75-kg) calf, for example, has to fill its stomach four or five times every day.

Bottle-nosed dolphins have even been seen teaming up with false killer whales (another type of dolphin) to attack sperm whales. Scientists are puzzled by this, because false killer whales also eat dolphins and dolphins can't eat sperm whales.

FISHING PALS

In Mauritania, the fishermen of the Imragen tribe are helped by bottle-nosed dolphins. The fishermen attract dolphins by hitting the water with sticks. The dolphins drive fish toward the shore, where other tribe members cast their nets to catch them. The advantage to the dolphins is that they find it easier to feed on the dense cluster of fish.

▲ These bottle-nosed dolphins are chasing a school of fish. The disturbance they create in the water helps to herd the fish closer together. Then they are easier to catch.

◀ Swimming together in schools helps fish reduce the chance of being eaten. It may also make it difficult for predators such as dolphins to pick out individual fish.

Dolphins often cooperate closely when hunting. Oceanic bottle-nosed dolphins herd fish together against the surface or into large fish "balls." Then each one takes turn feeding. In the Carolinas, bottle-nosed dolphins herd fish close to the shore, then rush at them. This creates a wave that washes the struggling fish onto the mud, closely followed by the dolphins, who nearly strand themselves.

Dolphins also feed individually and may dive to depths of more than 1,650 ft. (500 m). They chase fish by sight and echolocation, and can even find fish hidden beneath the sand. Dolphins can also flick fish out of the water with their tails. This stuns or kills their victims.

Adult Life

Bottle-nosed dolphins are probably the most widespread of all dolphins. They have adapted to live in many different habitats around the world and learned to catch and eat many different types of prey. Within its habitat, an adult dolphin has a home range. This is the area in which it spends most of its time.

▼ This adult bottle-nosed dolphin is blowing a trail of bubbles as it swims in its home range off the coast of Israel. A home range may cover hundreds of square miles.

▶ An adult dolphin's sleek, muscular body makes it an acrobatic swimmer. It is able to leap into the air and reach speeds of up to 25 mph (40 km/h) in the water.

Bottle-nosed dolphins living in cold waters grow larger than those in warmer waters. That is because they need more blubber under their skin to keep them warm. Living in such different habitats may someday lead to the division of cold- and warm-water dolphins. They may become separate species, unable to interbreed.

Breeding age

Females are able to breed between the ages of five and thirteen. Males can breed between nine and fifteen. Females that produce calves at an early age may not have the experience or sufficiently developed bodies to rear their calves successfully. On average, females become sexually mature at age ten and males at age twelve. Neither will reach their full adult size until two or three years later.

Finding a Mate

More male bottle-nosed dolphins die during adolescence than females. No one is sure why this happens. But it means that when the dolphins mature and leave their subadult groups, there are fewer males than females.

Alone, or with a few friends of the same age, the males travel widely between female groups. They search for opportunities to breed. At the same time, the newly matured females return to the maternal band in which they were born, living once again with sisters, mothers, and even grandmothers.

▲ Two bottle-nosed dolphins mate at the water's surface.

► These large male bottle-nosed dolphins are fighting for the right to mate with a female.

Courtship is accompanied by yelps and may involve chases. The pair jumps together out of the water, and they have lots of flipper contact. The dolphins usually mate in a belly-to-belly position. Male and female sexual organs are hidden away beneath slits along the belly. This is one reason it is difficult to tell the sexes apart.

Both males and females may mate with many partners. Mature female bottle-nosed dolphins usually have a calf every two to four years. They give birth mostly in late spring and early fall.

COMPETITION

Males compete with each other—often violently—to be able to mate with females. This may be why males have shorter lives. An individual male, or a small male group, may separate a female from her band and guard her from other males for many days while mating with her. During this time, another male or male group may try to steal the female away.

Lifespan

Life for a dolphin is much tougher than most people think. Finding enough to eat, keeping warm, and avoiding accidents or attacks from other marine mammals and sharks takes a heavy toll on a dolphin's health.

If a bottle-nosed dolphin survives into adulthood, it may live to between twenty-five and thirty years old if it is male. It may live up to fifty if it is female. The three major natural causes of death are parasites, disease, and predators.

STRANDED!

Cetaceans sometimes get stuck, or stranded, on beaches or sandbanks. This may be because their brains have been affected by parasites, causing them to become confused. Healthy animals may lose their way, fooled by unfamiliar coastal features. Some old or sick cetaceans may become stranded when they enter shallow waters for safety.

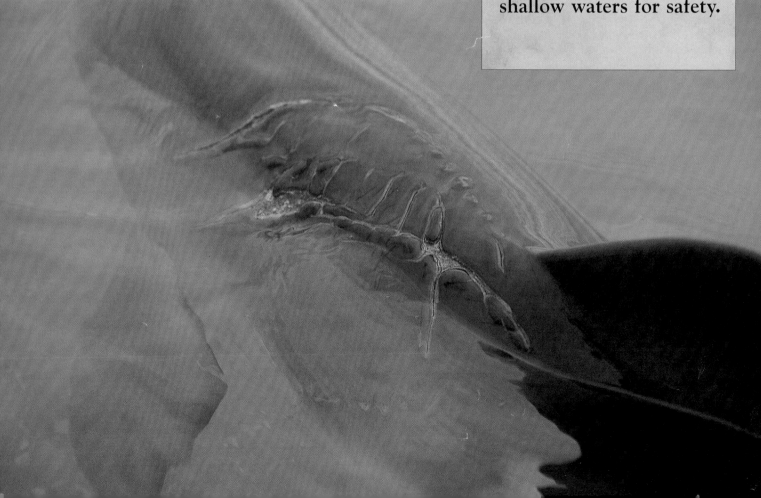

▲ When dolphins wash ashore dead, it is often hard to know why they died, unless there are obvious signs, such as fishing-net or shark-bite marks.

◄ Tiger sharks are fearsome predators. This bottle-nosed dolphin was lucky to escape alive from an encounter with a tiger shark, as the scars in its back show.

Dolphins' bodies are home to many parasites. Parasites are animals that live by feeding off other animals. They include tapeworms, nematodes, and flukes. These parasites do not usually cause serious harm to the dolphin's health. But if a dolphin is ill or very old, parasites can make it so weak that it dies.

Disease can spread rapidly among dolphins. In 1987, a virus killed at least 2,500 bottle-nosed dolphins off the southeast coast of North America. Sadly, there is evidence that many diseases are caused or made by pollution.

Dolphins and Humans

For centuries, sailors have enjoyed the sight of dolphins riding the bow waves of ships, often no more than an arm's length away. Until recently, ancient tales of dolphins befriending humans were thought to be no more than tall tales made up by seafarers.

Over the past fifty years, however, there have been many reports of individual dolphins settling in one area and seeking out human company. Most of them have been bottle-nosed dolphins. The dolphins, who love frolicking with swimmers, become local celebrities.

▼ Monkey Mia beach in Shark Bay, Australia, is home to several hundred bottle-nosed dolphins. Some of them, usually in small family groups, have been coming to the beach to meet humans since the late 1960s. The females trust humans enough to bring their young calves with them.

No one is sure if these dolphins are orphans or if they have simply been thrown out of their social group. Perhaps they are just curious dolphins who investigated a place and then settled there because it met all their needs.

Bottle-nosed dolphins, orcas, and other cetaceans are sometimes taken from the ocean and kept in marine aquariums. Many people now believe that such captivity is cruel, because captive animals suffer from stress, behavioral problems, and shorter lifespans. We can learn much more about cetaceans by watching them in the wild instead of in aquariums.

▶ This captive orca is performing in a marine aquarium.

35

Brain Power

In the 1960s, the American space agency NASA began to study dolphin "language." Unfortunately, no two-way conversation ever took place between humans and dolphins, but this research did reveal a lot about dolphins' brain power.

A dolphin calf's brain weighs 1.75 lbs. (0.8 kg) at birth. It continues to develop until the age of nine or ten—much longer than the brains of most other mammals. This is a sign that learning over a long period is important to dolphins, just as it is to humans.

▲ A researcher uses hand signals to communicate with captive dolphins.

◀ Are dolphins smart? Some of the things that dolphins do suggest that they may be very intelligent. Dolphins have learned to use use sea sponges to protect their beaks from sharp objects when hunting on coral reefs. They have also been known to skillfully undo fishing nets.

An adult dolphin's brain weighs approximately 4 lbs. (1.8 kg). Compared to its overall body weight, a dolphin brain is only slightly smaller than a human brain. The dolphin may need such a large brain to cope with its complex social life and senses, such as echolocation.

Research has shown that dolphins can use sounds to pass information to each other. They can also understand simple instructions. A dolphin can even be taught the difference between "take the ball to the hoop" and "take the hoop to the ball." But because dolphins live in an environment different from our own, the question Are dolphins intelligent? may never be answered.

Threats

Although the bottle-nosed dolphin itself is not at risk, human activities have put a number of cetacean species in danger of extinction. These include the Yangtze river dolphin, the Gulf of California porpoise, and the Northern right whale. Only a few hundred of each species are left.

Dolphins face different threats depending on where they live. The habitat of river dolphins, for example, is being changed by farming and large dams. Some dolphins are injured by collisions with riverboats. Others are caught in nets or poisoned by chemical waste dumped in rivers.

▼ A dolphin gets a free ride on the bow wave produced by a huge ship. But the noise of the ship's engines may end up harming the dolphin.

In some countries, dolphins are killed either for food or because local fishermen mistakenly believe they scare fish away. Even where they are protected, visits from well-meaning dolphin-watchers can upset the lives of wild dolphins.

Loud noises from oil exploration at sea, commercial shipping, and naval vessels may also be harmful. This noise pollution may alter the dolphins' behavior, and even affect their ability to hear. A further threat to cetaceans and other sea creatures is posed by global warming. This threat could change ocean temperatures and permanently alter Earth's weather.

▶ Oil and gas rigs can pollute the oceans by leaking or dumping toxic chemicals into the water.

Pollution and Fishing

Many chemicals dumped in the oceans are absorbed by tiny marine animals at the bottom of the food chain. The chemicals become more concentrated in animals farther up the chain.

By eating other marine animals, dolphins receive highly concentrated amounts of pollutants that are eventually stored in their blubber. When a dolphin is sick or producing milk, it breaks down blubber to provide extra energy. This frees the pollutants, which can damage the dolphin's fertility and its ability to fight diseases. A mother passes huge quantities of these pollutants to her calf through her milk.

▲ For all their amazing abilities, wild dolphins can't swim backward. If they get caught in a net, there's no way out.

▶ Fishing vessels, such as this trawler, catch over 100 million tons of sea life each year—more than the sea can naturally replace. Dwindling populations of sea creatures will reduce the food available to cetaceans. This may threaten their survival.

TUNA FISHING

Over the last 30 years, 7 million dolphins have been killed by tuna fishing in the eastern Pacific Ocean. Yellowfin tuna often swim below schools of dolphins. The tuna fishermen know that if they net the dolphins, they are likely to catch the tuna as well. Consumers can help dolphins by buying "dolphin-friendly" tuna. This tuna has been caught with fishing lines rather than nets, so it causes less harm to dolphins.

Fishing is another danger. Each year, many thousands of dolphins and porpoises die when they get tangled in fishing nets. Some nets, such as drift nets, are hard for dolphins to see. Others, such as trawl nets, may be used in such a way that dolphins can't avoid swimming into them.

Protection

In the late 1960s, the "Save the Whale" campaign made people aware of just how many whales were being hunted and how cruel the hunting methods were. The public then discovered that large numbers of dolphins were dying in tuna nets in the United States. The result was the 1972 Marine Mammal Protection Act. It has done much to protect marine mammals in U.S. waters. Since then, several other countries have also introduced laws to preserve marine mammals and their habitats.

▼ Educational dolphin- and whale-watching trips allow many people to enjoy the sight of cetaceans in the wild. Conservationists are drawing up guidelines to ensure that such trips disturb the animals as little as possible.

▲ Two bottle-nosed dolphins leap gracefully through the air. As scientists and conservationists learn more about the lives of these intelligent, beautiful creatures, we will also learn how to protect them better.

Fortunately, pollution is slowly being reduced, and stricter controls are being placed on fishing. A number of international agreements on pollution and fishing are now in place. Some are in the process of being set up.

You can find out about organizations working to save dolphins and other cetaceans on page 47.

Dolphin Life Cycle

Following a twelve-month pregnancy, a dolphin mother usually gives birth to a single calf. The calf is able to swim right away, and it sometimes has to drink its mother's milk on the move.

 For the first week, the mother and calf are always together. The calf soon begins to swim on its own. It is looked after by female relatives while its mother goes off hunting.

 Weaning begins as early as four months, but the calf keeps on drinking milk until it is eighteen months old. The bond between mother and calf will be strong for several years.

4 Between three and six years of age, the juvenile dolphin leaves its maternal band. It joins a sub-adult group, which includes the friends it has grown up with.

5 Females mature between five and thirteen years old. Males mature later, at about the age of twelve. The females return to the bands in which they were born. Males go off in search of females with whom they can breed.

6 Females have a calf every two to four years and may continue to breed into their forties. Females may live for up to fifty years. Males usually reach only their early thirties, perhaps because of violent clashes with rival males.

Glossary

Adolescence The stage of development between a young animal and an adult.

Blubber A layer of fat under a dolphin's skin that keeps it warm.

Cetacean A dolphin, porpoise, or whale.

Courtship Behavior that leads to mating.

Crustaceans A group of animals with a hard outer body casing and jointed limbs.

Echolocation The way dolphins use sound to locate prey and find their way around.

Evolved Developed slowly over time.

Extinction The dying out of a species.

Global warming The gradual warming of Earth's climate caused by pollution.

Habitat The natural home of a species.

Infanticide The killing of young animals by older members of the same species.

Interbreed To breed together.

Mammals Warm-blooded animals that produce milk for their young.

Mammary glands Parts of a female mammal's body that produce milk.

Noise pollution Harmful noise in an environment.

Parasites Animals or plants that live in or on another animal and feed off it.

Polluting Spoiling the environment with harmful chemicals and gases.

Predator An animal that hunts and kills other animals (called prey) for food.

Slipstream The current of water produced by a boat or a swimming animal.

Social status An animal's rank, or level of importance, within a group.

Species A group of animals or plants that are able to breed with one another.

Tall tale A story told many times that is not necessarily true.

3-D Three-dimensional, or lifelike.

Ultrasound A technique that uses pulses of sound to create an image.

Umbilical cord The tube that connects a mammal mother to her unborn baby.

Weaning The time when a calf stops drinking milk and starts eating solid food.

Further Information

Organizations to Contact

American Cetacean Society
P.O. Box 1391
San Pedro, CA 90733-1391
www.acsonline.org

The Dolphin Institute
1129 Ala Moana Boulevard
Honolulu, HI 96814
(808) 593-2211
www.dolphin-institute.com

Whale and Dolphin Conservation Society
Alexander House
James Street West
Bath BA1 2BT
UK
www.wdcs.org

World Wildlife Fund
1250 Twenty-Fourth Street, N.W.
P.O. Box 97180
Washington, DC 20077-7180
www.worldwildlife.org

Books to Read

Berger, Melvin. *Do Whales Have Belly Buttons?: Questions and Answers About Whales and Dolphins.* Scholastic, 1999.

Carwardine, Mark. *Whales, Dolphins and Porpoises.* Time-Life Books, 1998.

George, Twig C. *A Dolphin Named Bob.* Harpercollins, 1996.

Grover, Wayne. *Dolphin Freedom.* Greenwillow, 1999.

Parish, Steve. *Dolphins.* Gareth Stevens, 2000.

Parker, Steve. *Whales and Dolphins* (Look Into Nature). Sierra Club Books, 1994.

Pascoe, Elaine. *Animal Intelligence: Why Is This Dolphin Smiling?* Blackbirch, 1998.

Wu, Norbert and Leighton Taylor. *Dolphins.* Lerner, 1999.

Index

Page numbers in **bold** refer to photographs or illustrations.